Title

But Criminalization is Selective: A Comprehensive Reasoning

Oligarchic Partiality in Formulating Crime

Copyright

Dedication

To the **redoubtable** God I dedicate this work for the Lord is my Guide and Guardian who surrounds me with Grace, Prosperity and Righteousness. I thank God for the Gift of Confidence imbued in me, and the Peace enveloping me as a result, even in adversity. I appreciate God for the Fearlessness with which I Delight in life because the Lord is with me at all times and always Comforting me. I am forever Grateful to God for allowing me the Joy of living and Glory everlasting. I Dance to the Lord's Showers of Goodness and Mercy as I am Elevated above those who seek to injure me. I am Proud in my acceptance of belonging to God and Happy in knowing that the Lord is for, and at, all times my Sanctuary. I love the Lord God without Restraint for Never putting me in Want in the Periods in which I Lack. ©2009/2012/2013/2014

My secondary dedication goes to the *phenomena* of *crime*. These phenomena facilitate eternal discussions of the failures of the human mind.

Preface

Crime is a huge area of disagreement in concept and actual observation. As a concept *crime* attracts challenging definitions. The consequence of these challenging, and at times fresh, definitions of *crime* is that *crime* is not a phenomenon in the sense that we have a set of behaviours we can universally agree as constituting *crime*. *Crime* is a collection of *phenomena* in the varied ways we observe *crime* being displayed. There is *crime* as the *social prohibition*. There is also *crime* as the *moral abhorrence*, and of course there is the ubiquitous *crime* as the *legal circumscription*. As a result, *crime* is more than the *apparently-definitive* legal circumscription determined by the criminal justice system (CJS) all over the world. However, it is *crime* as defined in legal terms by the CJS - all over the world - that is much discussed. Yet, the moral *crime* and the social *crime* offend human sensitivity, at times much more than the legally condemned *crime*.

We are safe to believe that the *normative moral crime* and the *normative social crime* form the basis of legal *crime*. As true as our belief is about the premise of legal *crime*, we might or might not be conscious that the normative moral *crime* and the normative social *crime* underpinning our legal *crime* are *segregational*. This segregation of what and/or which aspects of the moral and social *crime* should formulate the legal *crime* is founded on the preferences of those in Government whether we have ushered them in as our representatives through the ballot box or they have bulldozed themselves in through the barrel of a gun. In this way, the formulation of legally prohibited *crime* is through *oligarchic partiality*.

As a rule the **invariable** foundation for the determination of the legal *crime* should be **stood** on the moral *crime* and the social *crime* disturbing our sense of confidence, assured safety and evident security, as 'The People'. This process of determination is **universal** for, and to, us as 'The People'. Thus, the universal normative moral *crime* and the normative social *crime* should **underscore** what conduct to criminalize in a progressive society. Having this understanding of the universal normative moral *crime* and the universal normative social *crime* as the **bases** for the universal legally proscribed *crime* should enable us to move forward *confidently* and *acceptably* to formulate legal *crimes* which arise from the expectations and *will* of 'The People'. From here on, we can then proceed to genuine discussions on responding to such criminalized conducts. In short, *crime* should mean more than conduct **selectively** admonished by the penal code presided over by *oligarchic partiality*.

Abstract

The subject of this essay is reflected in its title. The title poses a disagreement with the end result of criminalization and claims the essay as a comprehensive reasoning on the processes of criminalization. The first part of the title "but criminalization is selective" states the essay's disagreement with the end result of criminalization and introduces two considerations. These considerations extend one another. One consideration is that the process of criminalization is **selective** about what that process determines as a *crime*. The second consideration is that the process of criminalization is **partial** - again *selective* - with the range of acts/conducts it embraces as *crime*, and/or would want to accept as *crime* within its already **restrictive** determination of *crime*. Thus, the main purpose of this essay is *encapsulated* by, and in, the simple question of "what is *crime*"?

The second part of the essay's title "a comprehensive reasoning" offers the essay as a **keen** examination of the processes of criminalization and attendant shortcomings. The essay explores some literature on *prevailing* discussions of crime and the practices of criminalization. This exploration brings us to the understanding that the determination of what is *crime* is **restricted** to legal formulation and the resultant *penal code*. Any conduct *insofar* as it is not within the *legal* proscription, no matter how *abhorrent*, is not *crime* and therefore not subject to criminalization and hence will not attract any *punishment*.

The essay finds that the process of the determination of *crime* necessarily follows from moral outrage and social indignation founded on the *preferences* of the representatives of the people elected into the legislature. At times, these so-called representatives of the people are self-imposed and they make law by **diktat**. Whether *appointed* into the legislature by election or *self-appointed* with the barrel of the gun, 'The People's' legislative representatives are *invariably* **oligarchic** and the choices they make for 'The People' are **underwritten** by *oligarchic preferences*. Inevitably, this essay concludes that the proper foundation for the determination of *crime* should encompass issues of *moral imperatives* and *social norms* (customs) – not moral outrage and/or social indignation – important to 'The People' rather than the codifying of *oligarchic preferences* of 'The People's' legislative representatives (ushered in by the vote or self-imposed by means including the barrel of the gun and/or the concerted and well-orchestrated calculations of the minority masquerading as the voice of the majority).

Contents

1   Introduction

The problem of *crime* is of perennial concern and it always ignites disagreements. These disagreements, however, overshadow the greater questions of *crime*. Note that I have used the expression "of crime" rather than "about crime". This is because the evident disagreements are about responses to the person committing a *crime*. Thus, these disagreements presume that we are all agreed on the existing identifications of *crime* and criminal conduct thereof. Yet, the disagreements are constrained to the legal definition of *crime*, that is, conduct proscribed by the penal code. What we know to be a *crime* is what the law says is a *crime*.

We note that our understanding of *crime* is rooted in what the law defines and/or describes as a *crime*. When we are ordinarily, therefore, told that "a crime has been committed", we know exactly what is meant. At least, we assume that we know because our minds go directly to the criminal justice system (CJS) and what we understand within the system as a *crime*. While we might not yet be aware of the precise *crime* committed we are not mistaken in our minds that it is a breach of the penal code.

When we hear someone say "that is a crime". We are not sure what is meant unless we share the same social consciousness with the person who has made the claim. We are not sure, ordinarily, because we are unable to recognise the act (or conduct) claimed as a *crime* as breaching the penal code. We therefore look to the person making the claim to elaborate on why such and such acts are a *crime*. We might then accept that person's explanation or resist it or even reject it.

When we say "but that must be a crime". Again, some of us hearing the statement might be confused as to what is meant. We perceive, however, that the person making the statement is appealing to our moral conscience and maturity. S/he is apprising our moral conscience that the act in question ought to be classified as a *crime* under the penal code. S/he is also at the same time arousing our moral maturity to the fact that the act in question does not fall foul of the penal code.

The primary purpose of this essay is to contribute to the debate on legal criminality and the twin issues of (i) selective criminalization of certain acts vis-à-vis the non-criminalization of equally, if not more repulsive acts, and (ii) the sanctity of the *inalienable* right of the individual. Although legal criminality is a universal issue in the sense that the criminal justice system (CJS) exists in almost every part of the world, the essay focuses on the discussion around legal criminality in the Western world. There is a simple reason for this focus. The author is reasonably conversant with the discussion and practice of legal criminality in the Western world but not at all familiar with such discussions and practices in other parts of the world[i].

2   What is *Crime*?

Crime, however it is defined, is a breach of the penal code (of any country). This explanation of mine of *crime* is straightforward but what is a 'penal code'? The 'penal code', also known as the 'criminal code', is compilation of acts which are considered as harmful by law and which attract punishment imposed by law according to the severity of the harm caused. Here too, my explanation of *crime* as understood by, and in, the 'penal code' is quite easily digestible. I have provided this definition as the *consequence* of the *prevailing* understanding - all over the world, by the way - of what *crime* is. This understanding of *crime* is quite a restrictive identification of what constitutes *crime*. Simply stated, it is an understanding that if an act, otherwise conduct, is proscribed by the penal code then that act or conduct is a *crime*.

I contend that *crime* should mean more than conduct admonished by the penal code. For a start, I would like to anchor my contention in the initial origin of the word *crime*. The expression *crime* itself is Old French but is traced to the Latin *crimen* meaning *judgement* or *accusation* or *offence*.[ii] What sense do we gather from any of these three interpretations of *crimen*? *Judgment* entails the expectations of *restitution* and/or *retribution* so do *accusation* and *offence*. The penal code is restitutive although not obviously so but is *evidently* punitive. Thus, from the penal code we understand the expression *crime* to have *exclusive* connection to *harmful* conduct which, in turn, attracts punishment. We can now ask ourselves if the penal code encapsulates the total extent, or even reasonable extent, of punishable acts, i.e., *harmful* conduct? I would say not. The penal code is *partial*. I use 'expression' rather than 'word' to identify *crime*. A 'word' can simply represent a description whereas an 'expression', as a matter of course, represents a description and an explanation. Thus, when we say *crime* we are describing an event as well as explaining that event. In order to pursue my contention we require a working definition that would serve that contention comprehensively.

As Voloshinov argues, language can be shared in use and yet have different meanings for users because "differently oriented accents intersect in every ideological sign".[iii] Thus, certain words in a language have a multiplicity of accents informed by the user's ideological position or social understanding. *Crime* suffers from this multiplicity of accents. Depending on one's ideological position, *crime* could refer strictly to legally proscribed conduct[iv] or expansively to any abhorrent conduct whether or not legally circumscribed.[v] In the expansive sense, criminal conduct would include such conduct that is socially prohibited by cultural norms. In the same expansive sense, criminal conduct would refer to morally abhorrent conduct. In fact, all legally proscribed *crimes* are predicated on moral positions and here lies the problem. The morality that underwrites a legal proscription and/or legal acceptance at a given time is not always normative for society as a whole. For instance, the laws which legitimised both colonisation and slavery were founded on certain moralities, which only became superseded by the tide of time and events. Before these moralities were subsumed neither the colonised peoples nor the slaves bought into the moralities which colonised them or enslaved them.[vi]

While we know *crime* by what the law tells us *crime* is, to most of us, anywhere in the world, the issue of what is *crime* is more than 'what the law says is *crime*'. *Crime* is that unspeakable conduct, that is, **harmful act**, that interferes with our naturally given right to enjoy individual freedoms as human beings. This is my outright *comprehensive* definition for *crime*. This 'naturally given right' is *inexhaustible* insofar as its enjoyment does not obstruct enjoyment by another person. *Crime* is not, therefore, the simple legal description and proscription of certain behaviours. *Crime* is a conception underpinned by competing moralities. One; there is the legal morality that prescribes the penal code. Two; there is the social morality which is an articulation of social etiquette within a community or society. Three; there is the philosophical morality that is the essence of our view of nature and what we see as natural law. My recognition of these three types of *crime* is not novel because others have blazed that trail before me. However, my definition of *crime per se* is entirely my originality.

I would suggest a model for our comprehensive definition of *crime* to include the following: the natural right of the person to (i) fair treatment, (ii) security of own possession, (iii) safety of own person, (iv) reciprocating respect and (iv) choice of action. This operational model is *non-negotiable* inasmuch as the enjoyment of any by one person does not impinge that of another person.

3   Some Literature on the Discussion of *Crime*

3.1   In his paper, *Critical Criminology and the Concept of Crime*, Hulsman argues that criminalization presupposes a near-homogenous society of individuals, which (i) believes in and (ii) accepts a shared understanding of *crime* is. We understand Hulsman here to be referring to the penal code. We also sense him to be suggesting that the penal code *presumes* a universal agreement on what the punishment for crime should be. He is not necessarily proposing that we, as a matter of factly, believe in the impartiality of the penal code. Rather, his position is that we accept it only because we are resigned to its being forced upon us. Hulsman recognises our helplessness within the stranglehold of the penal code and this is why he maintains that the presumptions of shared belief and acceptance of the penal code are erroneous. In reminding us that substantial research has shown primary criminalization not to correspond to the "negativity of the situations" it is purported to "remedy"[vii] Hulsman clearly believes there is misfit between legally proscribed *crime* and the condition leading to such proscription. In other words, criminalization is not only *selective* but it is also *contrived*.

Hulsman goes on to propose that the CJS is directed principally at "the most disadvantaged sections of the population"[viii]. Hulman's argument here could be split into two essential parts. One part is implied in an obvious way and it is the argument that if an individual is of the working class, that individual is more likely to fall foul of legally proscribed *crimes* and to suffer the full wrath of the CJS. Hulsman is not arguing here that the working class person is more likely to commit *crimes*. What Hulsman is positing is that the CJS has been directed almost entirely at criminalizing the activities of the working class population. The other part to Hulsman's argument which is implied in a non-obvious way is that if an individual who has fallen foul of legally proscribed *crimes* were of minority origins[ix] and/or a woman and/or a member of the working class, that individual would suffer the full wrath of the CJS. Hulsman's position here is straightforward: the CJS is *sympathetic* towards an offender who is 'white', middle-class and a male.

3.2   Hulsman finds agreement in Fitzgerald and Sim. In *British Prisons*, they assert that not only does the CJS determines what conduct is criminal and prescribes sanctions against such conduct, it is also *partial* towards the middle classes in treating these classes "more leniently" than the working classes even for "similar offences"[x]. At any rate, they argue, most of the misdemeanours perpetrated by the middle classes are "governed by civil law"[xi]. This is a restatement that criminalization is not only selective but it is also contrived. In *Abolitionism: Towards a Non-Repressive Approach to Crime*, Bianchi also agrees with Hulsman in describing *crime* as social construction. For Bianchi the CJS is "*destructive*" because it abuses the "inalienable" rights of individuals[xii]. For him therefore, the CJS has no interest in *crime* control but exists *only* to perpetuate a power hierarchy.

3.3   Morris in *Persons and Punishment* disagrees with the argument of *crime* as a social construction and maintains that *crime* is an act committed by "those who have done what they had no right to do ..."[xiii]. In this way, Morris insists that *crime* is act *deserving* of its condemnation rather than act misconstrued to mean what it should not mean. Morris argues that human beings are bound by "primary ... rules that prohibit violence and deception" and that adhering to these rules ensures "benefits for all ... [such as] non-interference" with one another while at the same time imposing a "burden" on adherents, that is, those who toe the line[xiv]. It is the **mutuality** between *benefit* and *burden*, Morris maintains, that makes for a stable society. When a person relinquishes this burden, that person acquires "an advantage" over others[xv]. This advantage is *unscrupulous* and in its particular nature, it is a *crime*. *Crime* arises, therefore, according to Morris, from breaches of the "natural, inalienable and absolute right" of the person including "all moral rights"[xvi]. Morris advances a persuasive argument. He is correct to maintain that *crime* interferes with the natural right of the person but he is wrong to accept the penal code as *given*. For Morris to be convincing he has to resolve the contention by Fitzgerald and Sim that the misdemeanours of the middle classes are "governed by civil law". This problem is, in fact, an amplification of the *incoherence* of the Morris stance excluding middle class misdemeanour from being a "burden" on society.

3.4   Although von Hirsch in *Past and Future Crimes: Deservedness and Dangerousness in the Sentencing of Criminals* rejects benefits and burdens theory for its "arcaneness", for presuming perfect social orders, for weakness in articulating how *crime* is an "advantage"[xvii], his understanding of *crime* also appears to be morally expansive as Morris'. This expansiveness is *misleading* because it is just expansive but not *comprehensive*. von Hirsch believes that *crime* is "principally" a harmful act one should not commit "even in the absence of the state's prohibition"[xviii]. It is clear here that von Hirsch is appealing to our moral values. For him, criminal law regulates relations between persons by focussing on such "acts of intentional harm" and is thus a repository of "moral clues" for society[xix].

Morris and von Hirsch appear concerned with morality as a standard for criminalization yet their understanding of morality is *restricted* to the morality of the penal code. Their standard of morality is not comprehensive. I need to comment on an unfair, particularly puzzling criticism, of Morris by von Hirsch. von Hirsch tells us Morris is feeble on explaining why *crime* is an "advantage". If von Hirsch accepts *crime* as "principally" a *harmful act* that is prohibitive by nature, that is, natural law, how could it not be clear to him that a perpetrator of *crime* by the very fact of committing a *crime* against a person places the victim at a disadvantage? Would that *crime* not have denied the victim access to own property acquired for own enjoyment? Would the perpetrator, therefore, not have **secured** an "advantage" over the victim, the rightful owner of the property in question?

4 *Crime*: *Law*, *Moral Conscience*, and *Social Consciousness*

From our discussion of the existing literature on *crime* and criminalization, we can package the phenomenon of *crime* into three main categories. There is the category of *crime* as *social construction*. There is *crime* as *social interaction* in the thesis of "benefit and burden" exchange between members of society. There is also *crime* **narrowly** understood as harmful act by the CJS. All these various descriptions of *crime* have merits as well as demerits. Below are discussions of these merits and demerits, and how my definition, and model of *crime* fit into these discussions.

Let us remember my definition of *crime* as *that unspeakable conduct, that is, harmful act, that interferes with our naturally given right to enjoy individual freedoms as human beings* and the competing moralities of the (i) legal prescribing the penal code, (ii) social articulating social etiquette within a community or society and (iii) philosophical accentuating our view of nature and what we see as natural law.

Unless the requirements of both the social morality and the philosophical morality are embraced by the legal morality to be parts of the penal code it is clear to understand how and why these three moralities can be in conflict. They are not always competing because in certain ways social morality and philosophical morality facilitate the legal morality.

The philosophical morality is in simple terms the *moral crime*. It is the most harmful of the three categories of *crime* and the most *apparent* but the perennially *elusive* by choice in criminalizing.

4.1 Crime as Social Construction

The position held by Fitzgerald and Sim that the CJS is the tool by which the ruling classes perpetually restrict the activities and movement of the working class accords with Mathiesen's observation in *The Politics of Abolition* that imprisonment distracts "attention from the really dangerous acts" of the powerful[xx].

An example of "the really dangerous acts" of the powerful is in the following scenarios. One; and it is a *classic* example. It is the instance of a person sitting in judgement over a matter in which that person evidently has a 'conflict of interest'. It is not sufficient for that person to simply declare interest in the matter, that person must also in decency in accordance with natural law remove herself or himself from the matter. Two; equally as *typical* an example is the area of "contempt of court". This charge of *contempt of court* is none other than the *legitimized* oppression of the litigant by a Judge, and the elevation of the Judge, court, and court processes to the *plain* of the *omnipotent*. The presiding Judge is (i) the *complainant* of the *contempt of court* charge, (ii) the *Jury* of *contempt of court* charge, and (iii) the *punisher* (Judge) of *contempt of court* charge. That the notion of *contempt of court* exists in the first place is the worst form of criminality by the human against the human. It is quite simply a **forfeiture** of any respect the court process might seek from litigants *insofar as* **natural law** is the reference. Three; yet another example, and equally *perennial* as the foregoing, is the *absolution* of a presiding Judge from criminal offences while presiding on a case. A Judge outside of the court can be in breach of the penal code as much as the other person. When presiding over litigation or when judging litigation, a Judge cannot infringe the penal code yet this is the location of *most* abuse. This is where the unscrupulous Judge commits the most crime. This is where the Judge concocts and/or distorts and/or suppresses evidence in favour of one litigant against another.

Wood's argument in *The End of Punishment* that the assumption of the CJS as premised on "a given consensus", and of "individuals as moral equals and rational agents" [is] pure fantasy" against the "reality of social disadvantage, personal need, and emotional inadequacy" of offenders[xxi] clearly emerges from the consequences of the *insufferable* "really dangerous acts" of the powerful. However, Wood pulls together a number of conflicting sympathies, and appears *unreasonably* favourable to offenders than to victims. Woods, inevitably claims that it is not really the offender's fault that he or she offends. The actual culprits are i) the material circumstances of the offender and ii) the disposition of the offender.

Fitzgerald, Mathiesen, and Woods evidently represent the *crime* as *social construction* thinking and their concerns are, on the surface, questions of moral conscience. These concerns raise my occupation with moral *crime* and moral reflections on *crime* and how far these moral aspects of thinking about *crime* extend. We note from our commentators above that they see *crime* within the moral paradigm of the *oppressor* advantage over the *oppressed*.

It is correct, of course, that criminal law is not "a given consensus". It is easy to agree with this. If criminal law were "a given consensus" there would be no need for this essay arguing that criminal law is *selective* in promulgation as well as *restrictive* in its selectivity.

However, we must carefully extract from existing laws the protection offered the individual against the breach of that individual's *inalienable right* by another individual. This is the real issue. If a number of individuals share similar material circumstances and disposition, could we conclude from Wood's position that these individuals will act similarly without some form of prompting, i.e., peer pressure and/or fickleness and/or obsequiousness and/or outright bloody-mindedness and/or wilfulness, *et cetera*? Of course, we cannot make such a conclusion simply because of the ridicule of such a proposition. Could we say for instance, that every poor person without some other contributory factor is a thief or that every wealthy person without knowledge of that person's particular circumstances has acquired his or her wealth through duplicity? I would rather emphasise the culpability of the disposition of the individual[xxii]. It is this disposition that lays the individual open to some sort of prompting. This is where Wood has not carefully thought things through. He recognises the offender's disposition as partly responsible for that offender's conduct. However, he would rather wave off this disposition as *involuntary*. For Woods, the offender's disposition is not the offender's fault. Similarly, we cannot seriously argue that the criminalization of rape or burglary or killing without justification or maltreatment of persons, especially of children or paedophilia is socially constructed.

The claim of *crime* as a social construct denies the existence of conduct that is morally *prohibitive* because it infringes on the *inalienable rights* of those to whom such conduct is directed. Such affronts to persons and to feelings of security are not considered to be social constructions by victims. For the victims, their *suffering is real*. To recognise the real suffering of victims is not to deny that certain *crimes* are socially constructed or that the *crimes* of the powerful are **socially-deconstructed** into *no-crime* and therefore go largely unpunished.

4.2   *Crime as social interaction in terms of Benefit and Burden*

The benefits and burdens theory of *crime* fundamentally argues that there are codes within society beneficial for all, rich or poor. We find the rudiments of this theory in questions such as why must a person, irrespective of that person's social status, not have the right to the (a) privacy of own *home* without being burgled or (b) sanctity of own *body* without being raped or murdered? Even offenders appreciate the right to "noninterference"[xxiii]. We experience of offenders, and prisoners instituting grievance proceedings against the police, prison authorities within prison internal processes, probation within probation internal processes and/or with the courts for some *imagined* breaches of their rights. I say 'imagined' because by natural law, that is the 'state of nature', a person who *dismisses* or *abuses* the rights of another person *forfeits* any right to her or his own.

The advantage gained by the offender, that is the perpetrator, need not be *literal* as von Hirsch and others would demand[xxiv]. If a criminal act constitutes physical violence or the deprivation of another's property, a *psychological* advantage would have been secured in the former and a *material* one in the latter. A person does not gain an advantage by simply not paying heed to rules which are beneficial for all. If a person breaches the rules which *ipso facto* means harm is visited on another then the fact of that breach with its *attendant* gain, whether psychological or material *transforms* into an advantage.

Morris is a little less diligent in his expatiation of benefits and burdens theory of *crime*. He argues that criminalization prohibits individuals from doing what they have "no right to do" and that the CJS - his "justice" - restores the "equilibrium of benefits and burdens"[xxv]. Yet, his suggested expansive understanding of *crime* is **limited** to legally prohibited acts. Morris does not explain why some injurious acts to society, which distribute "unfair advantage" at their most basic such as environmental degradation and employers' negligence over the health of their employees, are not criminalized. Nor does Morris explain how such harmless acts as *prostitution* account to "unfair advantage".

Of course, there is an element of *unfair advantage* around *prostitution* but it is only *weighted against prostitutes* themselves. It is 'unfair advantage' to the detriment of *prostitutes* where they are forced into *prostitution* and kept in that activity against their will and/or under threat of harm by others. Female **sex workers**, more-eagerly referred to as *prostitutes* also face possible or probable harm from male clients. Interestingly, some 'moralists' would argue that *prostitution* is unfair advantage to the detriment of communities where *prostitutes* plying the streets are *blight* and an *encumbrance* to community life. On the face of it, this argument has substance: who, for example, would not find it offensive for their teenage daughter to be propositioned by a man looking to sleep with a *prostitute* because that poor teenager lives on the street plied by prostitutes? In reality, the argument fails to recognise the intrusion of the law on the independence of the person, this time a woman,[xxvi] to do whatever she wants to do with her body for as long as she causes no harm to another person.

The possibility that *prostitution* is blight and an encumbrance to community life is the consequence of the imposition of the law on the **inalienable rights** of *prostitutes*. What is the difference between a woman who has a number of bedfellows but does not charge them money and the woman who has a number of bedfellows but charges them money? The former is described in an offensive way at worst but transactions around the latter attract criminalization by men. We must not forget that it is men who defined the processes of courting a sex worker as *prostitution*, and then criminalized the transactions of this activity. The genesis of this criminalization was not *altruism* and its continuation is still not *self-less* but essentially predicated on *truncating* the freedom of the female sex worker savvy enough to make men pay for sleeping with her with "no strings attached". If activities around *prostitution* were to be de-criminalized and the public were to know that there is a *shop* they could legally go to and pay to sleep with a woman, we will not find our streets plied by unfortunate women who are themselves prey to unscrupulous handlers; the pimps.

4.3   *Crime as Harmful Act*

von Hirsch refers to Feinberg[xxvii] to present a hierarchy of harmful acts as acts which have breached, in descending order, the 'welfare interests', 'security interests' and 'accumulative interests' of others[xxviii]. Feinberg himself argues that "the capacity to engage normally in social intercourse and to enjoy and maintain friendships, at least minimal income and financial security, a tolerable social and physical environment, and a certain amount of freedom from interference and coercion. ... [are] minimal but nonultimate goals [which] can be called a person's 'welfare interests'"[xxix]. Borrowing from Feinberg's explanation of welfare interests, von Hirsch breaks "welfare interests" into two: the physical and the economic. To breach either the physical or the economic interest, according to von Hirsch, is to inflict serious harm.

von Hirsch's suggested expansive understanding of criminalization, as with Morris, is limited to legally proscribed acts. He explores harmful acts only in respect of acts prohibited by criminal law. If harmful acts are acts which should not be perpetrated even in the absence of legal proscription, and if criminal law makes certain that these acts are not committed at all, why is it that some of the most dangerous acts of all: (i) the pollution and (ii) the degradation of the environment are not as a matter of rule criminalized by this criminal law that seeks to punish "acts of intentional harm"? Or is it just possible that von Hirsch does not see the pollution and the degradation of the environment as "acts of intentional harm"? Treaties on environmental pollution do not suggest that these acts are not intentionally harmful. In fact, in some jurisdictions such as the US, environmental pollution is criminalized to a certain extent. von Hirsch is familiar with such jurisdictions.

Rescher's treatment of *welfare interests* is an earlier and a more comprehensive exposition from which both Feinberg and von Hirsch borrowed. Rescher proposes a third aspect of welfare interests a breach of which also is to inflict serious harm. This is what Rescher says regarding this third aspect which he identifies as "psychological": "Welfare is a matter of the basic requisites of well-being, and a man is so constituted that he cannot achieve this condition without reference to the condition of those about him. ... A threat to the welfare of his family and his friends is transmitted through the linkages binding them together to become a threat to his own welfare as well"[xxx]. Translated literally, Rescher comments that if an individual's family and/or friends are threatened so is that individual. In a broader sense, by recognising the psychological dimension to welfare interests, Rescher suggests that any harm done to an individual is not restricted to that individual but is extended to that individual's family, friends, and work colleagues. In this way, an offender has not just harmed the single individual at whom the harm has been directed but a network of individuals connected to that single person to whom the initiating harm has been directed. Rescher's proposition is so obviously evident. For instance, where a person was robbed of property, would the offender not have deprived the victim's family the right of enjoyment to that property? We can also consider where an individual has been raped. Would such an ugly act not impact on the personal relationships of the victim to the extent that distress is caused all around? Or if an individual were maimed or murdered, is the impact of such an ugly act on the lives of those close to the victim so difficult for us to imagine?

5   Criminalization and the Minority person

Although academic discussions of *crime* for the most part do not specifically focus on the political implications of the CJS for members of minority communities save for largely sociological considerations, we can deduce how a system that discriminates essentially against the working classes would impact on minority members of society. Minority members are even more excluded from the sympathies and benefits of societies, which until recently, have taken them for, and treated them as, subspecies.

To argue that the CJS in the Western world is riddled with racism is to reiterate an enduring proposition. The proposition does not presume that the Western world has a monolithic CJS. It is simply stating that irrespective of the complexion of the CJS in different parts of the Western world, the CJS is saturated with prejudice against those individuals and/or groups that are seen as the *other* in general and the *other* in particular. One is the *other* in general where one is of a different **social class** to those in the CJS making decisions about one. One is the *other* in particular where one is of a different **racial identity** to those in the CJS making decisions about one. This proposition of the *other* is enriching in two important ways. One, it requires us to identify the constituents of the CJS. Two, it enables us to identify what role each constituent plays within the racial discrimination process of the CJS. The constituents of the CJS, of course, comprise the Police as the first point of contact, the prosecution service as the second port of call, the criminal courts as the third venue in the process where the *labelling* of the individual as a criminal effectively takes place and, the prison and the probation service - separately or combined - as last points in the process where the *labelled* person now suffers the consequences of the labelling.

5.1   *The Police Service as a Constituent of the CJS*

A random count of any police service population in the Western World will recount an overwhelming proportion of Occidentals ('whites') vis-à-vis the general population ant which way one looks at it; (i) proportion by racial percentage of the general population, (ii) proportion by educational qualifications of the general population, (iii) proportion by gender representation of the general population.

5.2   The Prosecution Service as a Constituent of the CJS

A chance observation of any prosecution service population in the Western World will recount an overwhelming proportion of Occidentals ('whites') vis-à-vis the general population any which way one looks at it; (i) proportion by racial percentage of the general population, (ii) proportion by educational qualifications of the general population, (iii) proportion by gender representation of the general population.

5.3   The Criminal Court as a Constituent of the CJS

A random experience of any criminal court in the Western World will recount an overwhelming proportion of Occidental ('white') males as Judges vis-à-vis the general population any which way one looks at it; (i) proportion by racial percentage of the general population, (ii) proportion by educational qualifications of the general population, (iii) proportion by gender representation of the general population.

5.4   The Prosecution Service as a Constituent of the CJS

A casual contact with either the prison service population or probation service population in the Western World will recount an overwhelming proportion of Occidentals ('whites') vis-à-vis the general population any which way one looks at it; (i) proportion by racial percentage of the general population, (ii) proportion by educational qualifications of the general population, (iii) proportion by gender representation of the general population.

5.5   Indelible Impact of the CJS

5.5.1 All the stages of the CJS enjoy incredible levels of *discretionary power*. By the very fact of its *selective application*, discretionary power allows *whimsical display* by the individual with that power. Thus, it is particularly imperative to remove discretionary power in the application of criminal justice in order to eliminate racial prejudice within the processes of the CJS. If there are set standards it will be pretty hard for any part of the CJS to breach those standards without being exposed. However, it is fair to say that the first point of contact in the CJS is the most important in the criminalization process as it introduces the alleged offender to the whole gamut of the system. This is where the **whimsical** application of *discretionary* power is most crucial because it is the location in the CJS where *most injury* is caused to minority individuals. Thus, the discretionary power of the Police in *ensnaring* individuals into the criminal justice labelling net is the most *resonant* of the discretionary powers existing within the CJS. After all, if the Police do not pursue a case that case does not get handed to the prosecution service and which, in turn, would not progress the matter to the criminal courts.

5.5.2 An examination of the interface between minority persons and the Police can rightly point us towards an understanding of *how*, *when*, and *why* minority individuals come in contact with the CJS as 'lawbreakers'. In some jurisdictions, the Police are *operationally* racist. This operational racism explains the *why* minority persons become criminalized and it underpins two scenarios. One scenario suggests that the Police deliberately set out to target minorities in their normal day-to-day *operational activities* such as patrols. This suggestion is not without foundation. Research on policing in Western countries confirms such *selective policing* of minority populations particularly the so-called blacks. A classic illustration here is the phenomenon of "driving while black" when black motorists - particularly male - are stopped by the Police for driving expensive cars. In the eyes of Police officers a 'black' person driving an expensive car is *prima facie* a criminal. Another infraction against the inalienable right of the 'black' person which has not attracted as much attention as driving while black is another phenomenon closely related. I will call this phenomenon *walking black in a rich neighbourhood*. This is when 'black' persons - again, mostly male - are stopped and searched while walking in – or are in the vicinity of - wealthy and mostly 'white' neighbourhoods/areas[xxxi]. I will call these two phenomena of (i) 'driving while black' and (ii) *walking black in a rich neighbourhood* the **concerted** type of **selective policing**. It is **concerted selective policing** because it is deliberate **racist policing**.

5.5.3 The other scenario of operational racism implies that Western Police forces treat minorities harshly and disproportionately even where law enforcement obligations are evidently incumbent on the Police. This is what I have identified as the *accidental* type of selective policing. It is accidental because police racism does not come into effect until minority individuals have broken some sort of criminal law or are suspected of breaking such a law and the Police are under duty to respond to that breach at any rate. Thus, this second implication of racist policing recognises that those minority persons who come into negative contact with the Police would have committed or are suspected of committing or are suspected of attempting to commit a criminalized act. Thus, *accidental* **concerted selective policing** is predicated on two scenarios: (i) the *apprehension* of minority suspects and (ii) *response to emergency calls* by the Police involving minority persons in suspected misdemeanour.

5.5.4 The *accidental* type of **concerted selective policing** - *racist policing* - can be illustrated in the following manner. Let us imagine that the Police receive an emergency call or any other call that a gang of young persons are disturbing the neighbourhood. Let us further imagine that the Police then respond to the call by asking whether this gang is 'black' or 'white'. Let us now imagine that when the Police are told that the gang is 'white', the Police do not despatch officers immediately to the scene but allow some cooling-off period. Let us then imagine that when the Police are informed that the gang of young persons disturbing the neighbourhood are 'black' that the Police react by arriving at the scene almost with alacrity. Such Police discrimination of response to the same event perpetrated by different ethnic groups would explain generally the *when* and *how* minority persons are entangled in the criminal justice *labelling* net.

5.5.5 Thus, the same explanation of the selective racist policing - *concerted* or *accidental* - of minority individuals elaborates the *how*, the *when* and the *why* minority persons become criminalized within the Western CJS. And the first turn of the wheel of the accidental type of selective racist policing of the minority individual begins when the Police on receiving the call of a disturbance by a gang of young persons ask whether this gang is 'black' or 'white'. Indeed, one could argue that this response is also of the concerted type of racist selective policing. However, it is more of the accidental type because a call reporting a disturbance by a gang of young persons comes in as an *off chance*, irrespective of its frequency, and the on-the-spot decision to ask that *most irrelevant* question of whether the gang is 'black' or 'white' is taken at the discretion of officers who receive the report.

5.5.6 In explaining the particular question of *when* minority persons get snared in the criminal justice *labelling* net, it is supposed that the minority person would have committed or is suspected of committing or is suspected of attempting to commit a criminalized act. However, in the illustration given above, a gang of 'white' young persons would also have committed or suspected of committing or suspected of attempting to commit a criminalized act. Yet, this gang of 'white' individuals has not been brought into the criminal justice labelling net because the Police allow enough time for the gang to disperse. The Police would know that the gang would disperse if the person who reported that gang's activities to the Police had threatened the gang with Police presence but that it would take that gang a few minutes to scatter because its members would want to exhibit some braggadocio towards the concerned individual. Not only would the Police have allowed these 'white' young persons to get away with attempting to commit an offence or with committing an offence, the Police would also have squandered the opportunity to identify active individuals in the 'criminal' fraternity. In this way, the Police would have deliberately *skewed* the picture of criminal activities and the players.

5.5.7 The particular question of *how* minority persons get tangled in the criminal justice labelling net is explained equally with the same conditions which explain the *when*. In dispatching officers immediately to incidents where a gang of 'black' young persons are congregated, the Police are able to apprehend such individuals in the act of committing or attempting to commit a criminalized act. Further, the Police might also be able to identify individuals active in other 'criminal' activities. What we then have is a situation where the Police are consistently able to *stigmatise* the 'black' population (or any other minority population that is the focus of attention in a jurisdiction) as more criminally active than other populations because the Police have the figures to show for it. After all, it is all a question of visibility (and statistics[xxxii]) . What the wider public would not know is that it is the Police organisation itself that is manipulating these figures to present an erroneous and racist picture with its strategy of selective racist policing - *concerted* or *accidental*.

6   Conclusion*:* The Inalienable Right of the Person is Absolute

The discussion of *crime* and criminality should be a discussion of the inalienable right of the person. If any aspect of this right is breached whether it is psychological or physical or economical/material then a *crime* against the person has occurred. This understanding of *crime* will include such interferences with the person through environmental pollution, environmental degradation and so forth. The environmental interference can be psychological as well as physical. Even the actions of Government[xxxiii] which are against the interests of the person but which are supposedly in the interests of the State - *raison d'état* - are *breaches* of the *inalienable right* of the person and are therefore criminal acts. The inalienable right of someone who breaches the inalienable right of another is not greater than that of the victim. And the pertinent question here really is: does the person who *disregards* the inalienable right of another not by that action *forfeits* his or her own too? The same consideration applies equally to an agency or body corporate or a Government that infringes on the *inalienable right* of the person.

The proposition of the CJS as a weapon of the ruling classes against the working class couched in legitimacy has two principal sides to it, both sides conflicting. In one respect, it is feasible to argue that not all crimes could be seen as criminalization of the activities of the working class, certainly not in the present times. However, the argument of the CJS as refuge of the ruling classes is not straightforwardly incoherent. It makes sense to argue that in the beginning the CJS served only the interest of the ruling classes. Let us examine the activities that were criminalized at the outset of the CJS. These activities were i) begging, ii) prostitution, iii) theft and its derivations: burglary, acquiring goods by deception, *inter alia*, and iv) murder. These clearly were activities that the working class person would have engaged in not because of a *naturalness* for a working class person to engage in them - what is natural for the working class person is equally natural for a person from the ruling classes if the same circumstances obtain - but because of the economic conditions of the working class person in those times.

Who would not beg under conditions of extreme hardship and where public-managed alms distribution was not readily available? Prostitution was clearly a live-saver for the working class. If one were not sure of where one's next meal would come from and/or where one would rest one's head for the night and alms of any sort were not obtainable, it would not take much of an imagination to recognise one's moral options without inflicting harm on another person. Where the working class person suffered abuse at the hands of the ruling classes: abuse such as refusal to pay the working person for a job done, *et cetera*, the working class person had no other natural recourse or any legal recourse for restitution other than to deceive the exploiter in order to secure the wage that was her/his rightful entitlement in the first place or to steal from the exploiter to compensate for her/his loss from the exploiter or if all else failed to kill the exploiter as a last act of desperation. The working class person may also have resorted to taking the life of the ruling class exploiter where the abuse suffered was ill treatment or rape of a female member of the working class where the CJS presumed a working class person naturally without integrity: who would take the word of a down and out person against that of a pillar of society?

However, in latter times, the above explanations of the criminal activities of the working class person are not defensible because of the contradiction between these explanations and the fact that working class offenders commit *morally and socially normative criminalized conduct* mostly against other working class persons. By *morally and socially normative criminalized conduct* I mean conduct as I have already mentioned such as burglary, killing without justification, paedophilia, rape, and robbery. Equally over time, the *crime* of theft and its derivations of burglary, acquiring goods by deception, and murder have shifted from being *afflictions* of the working class to being the afflictions of all classes.

In another respect, it is reasonable to accept the argument that the CJS is weighted against working class offenders - and offenders who are minorities - and who are unfortunate to be snared in the net. It is beyond debate that certain activities of the working class and/or minorities are criminalized while *comparably* atrocious acts by the ruling classes are not criminalized or that certain dangerous acts by the powerful are not at all criminalized or that certain acts committed by the working class have a higher hierarchy of criminalization than acts committed by the ruling classes. Typical of such an instance is the criminalization of crack taking and heroin taking in the US. The former is the preserve of working class African-Americans while the latter is the indulgence of affluent 'white' Americans. The former endures a Draconian sentencing - in fact, custodial sentences - whereas the latter attracts more or less a slap on the wrist.

It is also not unusual to find individuals in the UK criminally prosecuted for failing to pay their television licenses and put in prison for defaulting on court fines arising out of the television licence prosecution. Individuals are also put in prison as a rule for defaulting on court fines generally because such default is seen as contempt of court. When one is struggling to make ends meet, paying a licence fee every year for receiving British Broadcasting Corporation (BBC) programmes is hardly the most pressing demand on one's priorities. It is, in particular, an affront to one's sensitivity against the background that the licence fee goes towards paying fat salaries to staff in the BBC organisation that should be *self-sufficient* and *self-subsisting*. There are broadcasting enterprises not in any way reliant on the public purse. They are private concerns and their owners rake in incredible amounts of profit. If they can do it why does the BBC have an issue with going private? If private broadcasting is not responding to needs we would not have billionaire owners. The BBC can no longer call on the *sophistry* of the argument of programming responsibility to the British public. It is an argument that does not wash.

The fact of not being able to pay a fine arising out of the television licence prosecution is confirmation of one's poverty rather than a political statement. Importantly, putting individuals in prison for not paying court fines is a mind-boggler, going to prison for not paying a court fine? Wow, where is the dangerousness in not paying a court fine? On the other hand, corporate fraud, which is the preserve of the powerful and which is *very dangerous* - imagine the welfare rights of the many employees this activity would breach - goes largely without successful prosecutions all over the world.

Endnotes

---

[i]The author lives in the UK.

[ii]Hoad,1986.

[iii]Voloshinov, 1973, p.23.

[iv]See, for instance, Tappan, 1947; Sutherland, 1949; Wright, 1982.

[v]See, for instance, Mathiesen, 1974; Schwendinger and Schwendinger, 1970; Fitzgerald and Sim, 1982; Wright, 1982; de Haan, 1990.

[vi]I make this claim notwithstanding those indigenes who benefited from colonisation and the slaves who were not out in the fields and could not see a life beyond serving the Occidental ('white') master.

[vii]Hulsman, 1986, pp.30-31.

[viii]Ibid., p.27.

[ix]I have omitted the term 'ethnic' because of the presumption by the Occidental population - the 'white' population - that it is not itself an ethnicity. In reality, the 'white' population is also an ethnic population.

[x]Fitzgerald & Sim, 2nd edn, 1982, pp.24 & 124.

[xi]Ibid., p.24.

[xii]Bianchi, 1986, p.115.

[xiii]Morris, 1994, pp.38-39, original publication 1968.

[xiv]Ibid., p.33.

[xv]Ibid.

[xvi]Ibid., p.32.

[xvii]von Hirsch, 1985, pp.58-59.

[xviii]Ibid., p.56.

[xix]Ibid., p.48 & 51.

[xx]Mathiesen, 1974, p.78.

[xxi]Wood, 1991, p.66.

[xxii]See Kelly, 1955 on Personal Construct Theory, particularly the "fundamental postulate [of the theory and the] corollaries", vol. 1, pp.46-104.

[xxiii]See, for instance, Morris, *op.cit.*, p.33.

[xxiv]von Hirsch, p.58.

[xxv]Morris, *op.cit.*, p.34. See also Nozick, 1981, p.374 (on retributivism).

[xxvi]Prostitution as an act is not restricted to woman.

[xxvii]See Feinberg, 1984.

[xxviii]von Hirsch, pp.67-68.

[xxix]Feinberg, *op.cit.*, p.37. See von Hirsch, op. cit., pp.69 & 70 for his exposition of 'security interests' and 'accumulative interests', and Feinberg, *op.cit.*, p.270 for his exposition, particularly, of 'security interests'.

[xxx]See Rescher, 1972, p.5.

[xxxi]Interestingly, most urban young 'white' persons, especially males, nowadays walk 'black', talk 'black', dress 'black', sing 'black' and are 'black' in everything except that they appear 'white'. The perception, some might say, fact, of young 'white' persons as every bit 'black' in demeanour impulses the Police to 'pull them over' when in the vicinity of rich neighbourhoods. The occasions when the Police might not focus attention on these urban *walking black young white persons* would be when they are in poor neighbourhoods.

[xxxii]The statistics are used to justify the visibility but as social scientists we know that statistics do not as a matter of fact tell us about the value judgements, for instance, that underpin the collection of a particular set of statistics. Statistics only tell the story we want to

tell. At times, statistics serve to mask our inability to understand a particular problem or reason out responsible answers to particular questions.

xxxiiiGovernment is always mistaken for the State in academic literature but the two are not the same. The State is the embodiment of the people, the territorial boundary of which they are citizens and the Government of that territory. Government is simply the governing body of a territorial boundary and its people.

Bibliography

Barker, E. J,. 'The Paradox of Punishment: In the Light of the Anticipatory Role of Abolitionism', in Bianchi, H. & von Swaaningen, R. (eds.) *Abolitionism: Towards a Non-Repressive Approach to Crime*, Amsterdam: Free University Press, 1986.

Bianchi, H,. 'Abolitionism: Assensus and Sanctuary', (1986) in Bianchi, H. & van Swaaningen, R. (eds.) *Abolitionism: Towards a Non-Repressive Approach to Crime*, Amsterdam: Free University Press, 1986.

Bianchi, H,. 'Pitfalls and Strategies of Abolitionism', (1986) in Bianchi, H. & van Swaaningen, R. (eds.) *Abolitionism: Towards a Non-Repressive Approach to Crime*, Amsterdam: Free University Press, 1986.

Bottoms, A.E,. 'The aims of imprisonment' in *Justice, Guilt and Forgiveness in the Penal System*, Occasional Paper No 18, Centre for Theology and Public Issues (CTPI), Edinburgh: University of Edinburgh, 1990.

Braithwaite, J. & Petitt, P. *Not Just Deserts*, Oxford: Clarendon Press, 1990.
Christie, N., *Limits to Pain*, Oxford: Martin Robertson, 1982.

Cohen, J,. 'Incapacitation as a strategy for Crime Control: Possibilities and Pitfalls', in Tonry, M.H. and Morris, N. (eds.) *Crime and Justice: An Annual Review of Research*, vol. 5, Chicago: University of Chicago Press, 1983.

Cohen, S., *Visions of Social Control*, Cambridge: Polity Press, 1985.
de Haan, W., *The Politics of Redress: crime, punishment and penal abolition*, London: Unwin Hyman, 1990.

Duff, R.A., *Trials and Punishment*, Cambridge: Cambridge University Press, 1986.

Dunbaugh, F,. 'A Strategy for Abolishing Prisons in the United States', in Bianchi, H. & van Swaaningen, R. (eds.) *Abolitionism: Towards a Non-Repressive Approach to Crime*, Amsterdam: Free University Press, 1986.

Durkheim, E., *The Division of Labor*, New York: Free Press, 1964.

Feinberg, J., *Harm to Others*, New York: Oxford University Press, 1984.

Fitzgerald, M. and Sim, J. *British Prisons*, (2nd edn), Oxford: Basil Blackwell, 1982.

Greenwood, P. W., *Selective Incapacitation*, Santa Monica, Calif: RAND CORPORATION, 1982.

Hoad, T.F. (ed) The Concise Oxford Dictionary of English Etymology, Oxford: Oxford University Press, 1986.

Home Office., *Crime, Justice and Protecting the Public*, London: HMSO, 1990.

Hulsman, L,. 'Critical Criminology and the Concept of Crime', in Bianchi, H. & van Swaaningen, R. (eds.) *Abolitionism: Towards a Non-Repressive Approach to Crime*, Amsterdam: Free University Press, 1986.

Ignatieff, M., *A Just Measure of Pain*, London: Penguin Books, 1978.

Kant, I,. 'The Metaphysical Elements of Justice', from Murphy, J,. 'Marxism and Retribution', in Coleman, J. (ed.) *Philosophy of Law: Crimes and Punishments*, London: Garland Publishing Inc, 1994.

Kelly, G.A., *The Psychology of Personal Constructs*, (2 vols.) New York: W.W. Norton & Company INC, 1955.

Mathiesen, T., *The Politics of Abolition*, Oslo: Scandinavian University Books, 1974.

Mathiesen, T,. 'The argument against building more prisons', (1985) in Muncie, J. and Sparks, R. (eds.) *Imprisonment: European Perspectives*, Hemel Hempstead: Harvester Wheatsheaf, 1991.

Marx, K,. 'Capital Punishment', in *New York Daily Tribune*, 1853.

May, J. D., *REPORT of the Committee of Inquiry into the United Kingdom Prison Services*, London: HMSO, 1979.

Miller, W. B,. 'Lower Class Culture as a Generating Milieu of Gang Delinquency', *Journal of Social Issues*, 14, (1958) cited in Irwin, J & Cressey, D. 'Thieves, convicts and the Inmate culture', *Social Problems*, vol.10, no.1, (Autumn 1962).

Morris, H,. 'Persons and Punishment', in Coleman, J. (ed.) *Philosophy of Law: Crimes and Punishments*, London: Garland Publishing Inc, 1994.

Murphy, J,. 'Marxism and Retribution', in Coleman, J. (ed.) *Philosophy of Law: Crimes and Punishments*, London: Garland Publishing Inc, 1994.

Nozick, R., *Philosophical Explanations*, Oxford: Oxford University Press, 1981.
Rescher, N., *Welfare: The Social Issues In Philosophical Perspective*, Pittsburgh: University of Pittsburgh Press, 1972.

Rusche, G. and Kirchheimer, O. *Punishment and Social Structure*, New York: Columbia University Press, 1939.

Sutherland, E., *White Collar Crime*, New York: Dryden Press, 1949.
Schwendiger, H. and Schwendinger, J. 'Defenders of order or guardians of human right?', *Issues in Criminology*, 5 (2) (1970).

Tappan, P. W,. 'Who is the criminal'? *American Sociological Review*, 12 (1947).

Tonry, M,. 'Selective Incapacitation: The Debate over Its Ethics', in von Hirsch, A. & Ashworth, A. (eds.) *Principled Sentencing: Readings on Theory and Policy*, (2nd edn), Oxford: Hart Publishing, 1998.

van der Slice, A,. 'Elizabethan houses of correction', (1937) in Muncie, J. and Sparks, R. (eds.) *Imprisonment: European Perspectives*, Hemel Hempstead: Harvester Wheatsheaf, 1991.

van Swaaningen, R,. 'What is Abolitionism?', in Bianchi, H. & von Swaaningen, R. (eds.) *Abolitionism: Towards a Non-Repressive Approach to Crime*, Amsterdam: Free University Press, 1986.

Voloshinov, V.N., *Marxism and the Philosophy of Language*, New York: Seminar Press, 1973.

von Hirsch, A., *Past and Future Crimes: Deservedness and Dangerousness in the Sentencing of Criminals*, Manchester: Manchester University Press, 1985.

von Hirsch, A,. 'Selective Incapacitation: Some Doubts', in von Hirsch, A. & Ashworth, A. (eds.) *Principled Sentencing: Readings on Theory and Policy*, (2nd edn), Oxford: Hart Publishing, 1998.

von Hirsch, A. Bottoms, A.E. Burney, E. Wikstrom, P.O. *Criminal Deterrence and Sentence Severity: An Analysis of Recent Research*, The University of Cambridge Institute of Criminology, Oxford: Hart Publishing, 1999.

Wilson, James. Q,. 'Selective Incapacitation', in von Hirsch, A. & Ashworth, A. (eds.) *Principled Sentencing: Readings on Theory and Policy*, (2nd edn), Oxford: Hart Publishing, 1998.

Wood, C., *The End of Punishment*, Edinburgh: Saint Andrew Press, 1991.

Woolf, LJ., *Prison Disturbances*, April 1991, (Report), Command 1456, 1991.

Wright, M., *Making Good: prisons, punishment and beyond*, London: Burnett Books, 1982.

www.ingramcontent.com/pod-product-compliance
Lightning Source LLC
Chambersburg PA
CBHW051951280526
45789CB00009B/3261